Marshmallowville

Author: Dianna Rembert

Illustrator: Dianna L. McKinney

This book was created and designed by

Kendra S. Berni.

Author's Website:

www.big2455red.wix.com/author

<u>Acknowledgement</u>

Special thanks to my mother who is also the illustrator of this book. And a big shout out to my publisher, Kendra S. Berni. I couldn't have done it without the both of you.

<u>Dedication</u>

I want to dedicate this book to my supportive

family, especially my parents who created me.

Also my loving husband who always stands

by me and my eccentric ideas.

I love you all.

Marshmallowville is a sweet little town,

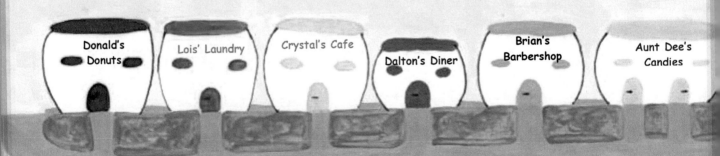

1

The streets are paved with creamy goo;
the trees curled chocolate brown.

The sky is filled with licorice drops
arching high above,

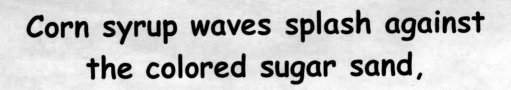

Corn syrup waves splash against
the colored sugar sand,

Boats designed of cream sticks are docked against the land.

6

Fish made from fudge swim through the Pudding Lake,

The moon is tasty taffy; the sun
baked out of cake.

Fences made of candy canes as far as
the eye can see,

Birds cut from cookie dough glide in
the air peacefully.

Bunnies covered in honey nibble on gummy carrots galore,

11

Gingerbread people smile and
wave at each and every store.

Trains roll on ice cream tracks;
quiet to the ear,

Cream-filled frogs croaking are all
that you can hear.

Bubble gum bumble bees buzz
in the spring time sky,

Brightly painted turtles live in shells made out of pie.

16

Cars are made of candy bars with
jelly doughnuts for each wheel,

17

Cats created from cotton candy;
dogs shaped out of oatmeal.

Lollipops are blooming where the flowers usually do,

Bicycles built of brownies using caramel for glue.

Close your eyes and think real hard
whenever you're feeling down,

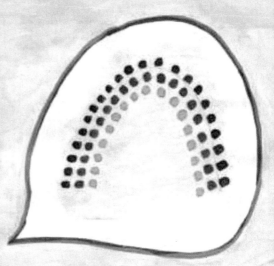

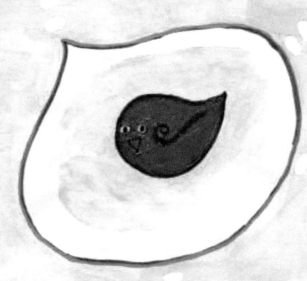

Dream about
Marshmallowville;
a very sweet little
town.

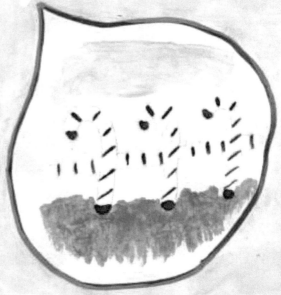

22

Remember all the yummy things that you just read about,

The warmth and joy that you feel will soon erase that pout.

Made in the USA
Middletown, DE
24 March 2016